Prayers, Decrees & Confessions for Healing

Apostle Stephen A. Garner

Copyright ©2016 Stephen A. Garner
PO Box 1545
Bolingbrook, Illinois 60440

All rights reserved. No portion of this book may be reproduced, scanned, or stored in a retrieval system, transmitted in any form or by any means – electronic, mechanical, photocopy, recording, or any other – except for brief quotations in printed reviews without written permission of the publisher. Please do not participate in or encourage piracy of copyrighted materials in violation of the author's rights. Purchase only authorized editions.

Unless otherwise indicated, all scriptural quotations are taken from the *King James Version* of the Holy Bible. All Hebraic and Greek definitions are taken from the *Strong's Exhaustive Concordance*,

ISBN 978-1539592433

Printed in the United States of America

Preface

This book is written to simply serve as a tool to help believers build a strong regiment of releasing a daily flow of wisdom into their lives by praying, decreeing and confessing the word of God. May you find hope and inspiration while praying, decreeing and confessing what you believe over your life, those whom you love and those to whom you are called is my prayer.

Table of Content

Introduction
Page 2
Circulatory System
Page 8
Cardio Vascular System
Page 14
Bones
Page 19
Muscular System
Page 23
Eyes
Page 28
Respiratory System
Page 33
Digestive System
Page 39
Immune System
Page 43
Endocrine System
Page 47
Nervous System
Page 54
Old Testament Healing Scriptures
Page 60
New Testament Healing Scriptures
Page 66

Prayers, Decrees & Confessions for Healing

Introduction

The first revelation that God gave to His corporate people, Israel, had to do with healing.

Exodus 15:26 KJV
And said, If thou wilt diligently hearken to the voice of the LORD thy God, wilt do that which is right in his sight, and wilt give ear to his commandments, and keep all his statues, I will put none of these diseases upon thee, which I have brought upon the Egyptians; for I am the Lord that healeth thee.

This was the first time that GOD spoke to HIS people as a whole and HE chose to reveal HIMSELF by HIS covenant name JEHOVAH RAPHA, the LORD our HEALER. GOD has made a covenant of healing with HIS people. First with Israel and now with the church.

Exodus 23:25 KJV
And ye shall serve the LORD your God, and he shall bless thy bread, and thy water; and I will take sickness away from the midst of thee.

3 John 1:2 KJV
Beloved, I wish above all things that thou mayest prosper and be in health, even as thy soul prospereth.

It is the will of GOD that HIS people live in divine health. When GOD created Adam and Eve, they were made perfect in the image of GOD. They lived in a state of perfection and divine health with every need taken care of. There was no sickness or death in Eden. As a matter of fact, GOD never designed for the human body to house sickness or infirmity of any kind. It was also never designed to die. This all changed when Adam sinned in the garden. With the entrance of sin came the entrance of sickness, disease, infirmities and death. The once immortal human body became mortal and susceptible to death.

Romans 6:23 KJV
For the wages of sin is death; but the gift of God is eternal life through Jesus Christ our Lord.

Sickness is a manifestation of death. If sickness was allowed to progress unhindered it would eventually lead to death. This is why before the invention of modern medicine many died of common ailments such as the flu. Sickness and sin both come from one common source; the devil. This is why GOD hates sin. The scripture says in *Acts 10:38:* How God anointed Jesus of Nazareth with the Holy Ghost and with power: who went about doing good, and healing all that were oppressed of the devil; for God was with him.

Sickness is the oppression of the devil. It is part of the master plan of satan for the destruction of mankind. It is evil and not the handiwork of GOD. Many have been taught by religion that GOD is responsible for sickness and somehow is glorified by the oppression of man. This could not be further from the truth. JESUS paid a horrible price to deliver us from sickness, disease and every manifestation of infirmity.

Isaiah 53:5 KJV
But he was wounded for our transgressions, he was bruised for our iniquities: the chastisement of our peace was upon him; and with his stripes we are healed.

Jesus went through unimaginable torture to secure our healing. Because of this EVERY believer has a right to walk in healing and to be healed. This was part of the reason why HE came.

Psalm 107:20 KJV
He sent his word, and healed them, and delivered them from their destructions.

JESUS not only came to save us from sin, but to deliver us from the things that would destroy us, such as sickness and infirmities.

1 John 3:8 KJV
He that committeth sin is of the devil; for the devil sinneth from the beginning. For this purpose the Son of God was manifested, that he might destroy the works of the devil.

Over seventy percent of the earthly ministry of JESUS was spent in healing the sick, casting out demons, performing miracles, signs and wonders. (see Matthew 8:1-2, 5-9, 13-17, 28-33)

Just as JESUS went about healing the sick, HE has given HIS church the power to do the same. Not only the church of the first century, but every proceeding generation has been commissioned by our KING to heal the sick.
(Mark 16:17-18)

It is time for the church in our generation to arise boldly in faith and exercise our kingdom mandate to go forth to heal the sick and walk in supernatural health. This book has been designed as a tool to equip you to do so.

Prayers, Decrees & Confessions for Healing the Circulatory System

Luke 8:43-44 KJV
And a woman having an issue of blood twelve years, which had spent all her living upon physicians, neither could be healed of any, 44 Came behind him, and touch the border of his garment: and immediately her issue of blood stanched.

1. I pray for purification in my blood plasma from all contaminants in Jesus name.

2. I decree the blood of Jesus Christ supersedes all issues that would seek to flow through my blood stream.

3. I renounce all generational proclivities that would defile my blood and I decree the blood of Jesus heals me.

4. I proclaim the power of God over my circulatory system and I decree the

marrow of my bones produce healthy blood only.

5. I renounce any issues with my blood as a result of poor circulation in Jesus Name.

6. I decree all disease common to vein collapsing and vein failures are forbidden from operating in my body in Jesus name.

7. I decree my veins carry a proper balance of oxygen to my heart and all blockages are rooted out in Jesus Name.

8. I confess excellence in my blood pressure. All hypertension is bound in Jesus Name.

9. I decree healthy levels of iron in my blood and all assignments of iron deficiency is healed in Jesus Name.

10. I decree my blood plasma produces the proper level of liquid in my blood in Jesus Name.

11. I renounce all assignments of coagulated blood and I decree blood clots are forbidden from forming in my blood. I proclaim divine anti coagulating power in my blood.

12. I proclaim strength over my health. I decree the life of my flesh is sound because my blood is pure.

13. I confess healing over all my arteries in Jesus Name.

14. I decree no arterial disease or ailment can prevail in my body for with the stripes of Jesus Christ I am healed.

15. I renounce all plaque and artery blocking infirmities in Jesus Name.

16. I confess the power of God over my arteries and I decree my arteries carry oxygenated blood with healing power from my heart throughout my body in Jesus Name.

17. Lord release a flow of Zoe life through my circulatory system and stimulate my blood to dominate all assignments of death in Jesus Name.

18. Life and vitality flow through me and my marrow is divinely producing blood cells free from any human weakness in Jesus Name.

19. Lord through your blood I decree the legalities of sin and sickness is broken off my health in Jesus Name.

20. I confess the Life Force of Christ over my health and I decree I will live out all my days in Jesus Name.

21. No blood sugar, poison or genetic disorder shall flow through my

blood. I decree my blood stream and blood flow is purified in Jesus Name.

22. All poor circulation is displaced and healing is flowing throughout my entire being.

23. I decree the fire of God manifest in my blood and the cold hands cold feet syndrome is broken in Jesus Name.

Prayers, Decrees & Confessions for Healing the Cardio Vascular System

Proverbs 12:25 KJV
Heaviness in the heart of man maketh it stoop: but a good word maketh it glad.

1. I renounce all diseases, symptoms, conditions and genetic disorders connected to my heart and cardio vascular system in Jesus Name.

2. I decree my heart is preserved and kept by Gods word from all infirmity and failure.

3. I confess the blood of Jesus over my heart and I command a cleansing from all vascular disease and deficiencies in Jesus Name.

4. I proclaim good health and I come out of agreement with any signs, symptoms and cardio vascular related problems in the Name of Jesus.

5. I confess my heart operates in a healthy range of beats per minute. (bpm)

6. I decree my arteries are off limits to any narrowing or shrinking. I renounce coronary artery disease in Jesus Name.

7. Father you hold the heart of kings in your hand. I decree my heart is held in perfect health by you in Jesus Name.

8. I decree my heart valves function properly and my blood flows without fail in the right direction in Jesus Name.

9. I renounce any leakage of my valves and I decree healing of my valves in Jesus Name.

10. I confess the virtue of God over my heart chambers and heart valves.

11. I confess the virtue of God over my heart chambers and heart valves.

12. I decree the upper and lower chambers of my heart work in perfect harmony.

13. Lord I ask you to expose any hidden congenital heart disease that would threaten my health in Jesus Name.

14. I confess your healing power over my heart and I decree divine order in the overall function of my heart in Jesus Name.

15. I renounce all pericardial disease. I decree the layers of the membrane of my heart operates properly in Jesus Name.

16. I cover my aorta in the blood of Jesus. I decree it supplies, without fail, oxygenated blood to my circulatory system in Jesus Name.

17. I confess your sustaining power over my heart. All degenerative disease is neutralized and perfect heart health is my portion.

Prayers, Decrees & Confessions of Healing for the Bones

Psalm 34:20 KJV
He keepeth all his bones: not one of them is broken.

1. Father cause your fire to manifest in my bones and destroy every assignment to make them brittle in Jesus name.

2. Lord break the power of all bone degenerating diseases in Jesus Name.

3. I renounce all osteoporosis against my skeletal system. It is destroyed in Jesus Name.

4. All inflammation and cartilage deterioration is forbidden from manifesting in my skeletal system.

5. I renounce all forms of arthritis that would cause inflammation of my joints.

6. I decree the assignment of arthritis fails in my hands, wrist, elbows, hips, knees, ankles and feet in Jesus Name.

7. Father cause your power to manifest through my vertebrae in Jesus Name.

8. I confess the healing power of God over my spinal column.

9. I decree no bulging disc will occur but creative miracles are being loosed upon my spinal column.

10. I renounce all brokenness of my bones in Jesus Name.

11. I renounce all rottenness of my bones in Jesus Name.

12. Lord release soundness in my bones and heal me of all bone spurs and bone fractures in Jesus Name.

13. I decree divine levels of salt calcium in my bones.

14. I renounce all demonic plans and agendas to promote infirmity in my bones in Jesus Name.

15. I proclaim God's power, over my bone marrow, releases strength into my entire skeletal system.

16. I renounce Paget's disease that would cause my bones to weaken in Jesus Name. I confess the strength of God over my entire skeletal system.

17. I renounce all cancers and infections associated with my bones and skeletal system is Jesus Name.

18. I decree life over my bones. I proclaim all genetic disorders are disallowed in Jesus Name.

Prayers, Decrees & Confessions for Healing the Muscular System

Job 10:11 KJV
Thou hast clothed me with skin and flesh, and hast fenced me with bones and sinews.

Ezekiel 37:6 Gods Word Translation
I will put ligaments on you, place muscles on you, and cover you with skin. I will put breath in you, and you will live. Then you will know that I am the LORD.

1. I proclaim God's strength and power over my entire muscular system. I decree healing and divine health over any muscular dystrophy disease in Jesus Name.

2. I renounce all congenital disease and infirmity rooted in muscle weakness, muscle deterioration and muscle failure in Jesus Name.

3. I decree all assignments that would affect my ligaments, tendons and sinews are displaced in Jesus Name.

4. I speak to any muscle spasms that would cause nerves to be pinched and cause me pain. It is neutralized through the blood of Jesus Christ.

5. I rebuke all assignments of Emery-Dreifuss (teenage males only) in Jesus Name.

6. I confess healing from all muscle related issues concerning my shoulders and arms in Jesus Name.

7. I speak proper growth over the muscles joined to my shoulders and arms. I renounce any symptom or signs of Emery-Dreifuss in Jesus Name.

8. I speak your healing power over all muscles locked into abnormal memory patterns due to injuries. I command all inflammation to cease and muscle tension to go in Jesus Name.

9. I command all knots and tightening of the muscles in my back to subside. I decree divine anti-inflammatory power over my muscular system in Jesus Name.

10. I renounce all muscle related issues that would negatively influence my nervous system. I command divine order between my muscle and nervous system in Jesus Name.

11. I speak alignment over my spine. I renounce all muscular problems rooted in spinal curvature in Jesus Name.

12. I decree that there will be no remote problems influencing my heart and respiratory system because of muscular dystrophy problems in Jesus Name.

13. I confess your power over all my facial muscles in Jesus Name. I decree there will be no contortions nor deformities in Jesus Name.

14. I decree Facioscapulohumeral (affects face, shoulder blade and upper arm bone) is neutralized through the blood of Jesus. I renounce any issues with my speech, swallowing or walking in Jesus Name.

15. I confess healing over my hips, all ligaments and tendons connecting that muscle group in Jesus Name.

Prayers, Decrees & Confessions of Healing for Eyes

Job 11:4 KJV
For thou hast said, My doctrine is pure, and I am clean in thine eyes.

1. I decree I have excellent eye health in Jesus Name.

2. I decree all assignments of vision related issues and diseases are neutralized through the blood of Jesus Christ.

3. I confess healing power over my cornea. I renounce all vision imparting symptoms rooted in Astigmatism that would cause irregular curves of my cornea. and cause blindness in Jesus Name. I'm healed of all fuzzy, blurry and distorted vision in Jesus Name.

4. I renounce diabetic retinopathy that would damage blood vessels of my retina and cause blindness in Jesus Name.

5. I command divine regulation of my blood sugar that would cause damage to my blood vessels and affect my retina in Jesus Name.

6. I decree all genetic and heredity disorders connected to glaucoma are broken off my life and healthy vision is my portion.

7. Lord manifest your power and heal me of all myopia or farsighted challenges. I proclaim excellence of vision in Jesus Name.

8. I pray for proper functioning of my optic nerves. I decree divine health over them and all degenerate disease that would affect the transmission impulses to my brain are bound in Jesus Name.

9. I renounce all forms of conjunctivitis causing detriment to my vision. All pink eye and allergies I command you to come out of my eyes in Jesus

Name.

10. I proclaim healing from any corneal abrasions as a result of foreign objects that flew into my eyes in Jesus Name.

11. I command healing of all eyelid inflammation due to infections and oil gland issues.

12. I pray for your power to manifest and address all dry eyes, red eyes, watery eyes, crusty eyes, swollen and itchy eyes in Jesus Name.

13. I renounce all eyelid problems. I decree any drooping and blinking spasms are bound in the Name of Jesus.

14. I decree divine detection of all problematic areas of my health connected to my eyes.

15. I renounce any forms of blurred or distorted vision and partial blindness. I decree you restore my sight.

16. Lord, root out all ailments that would cause inflammation of my arteries leading to headaches, facial pain and vision problems.

17. I renounce all color blindness and command proper functioning of retinal nerve cells.

18. I decree there will be no irregularities of my vision due to floating spots (aka floaters) in Jesus Name.

Prayers, Decrees & Confessions of Healing for the Respiratory System

Genesis 2:7
And the Lord God formed man of the dust of the ground, and breathed into his nostrils the breath of life; and man became a living soul.

1. Lord as you breathed into the nostrils of Adam and he became a living soul I ask that you breathe into me again and drive out all respiratory related sickness and disease in Jesus Name.

2. I renounce and come out of agreement with assignments against my trachea. I cover my windpipes in the blood of Jesus and command them to operate according to their divine design in Jesus Name.

3. I confess your healing power and virtue over my entire respiratory system in Jesus Name.

4. I pray against all asthma and problems connected and associated with it. I renounce all shortness of breath and allergy problems that would trigger asthma attacks in Jesus Name.

5. I confess victory over all fear and anxiety that would incite asthma attacks in Jesus Name.

6. I renounce all ungodly affects from asthma medication through steroids. I renounce all weight gain and any kind of eye related side effects in Jesus Name.

7. Lord I decree my respiratory system will not malfunction due to climate changes in Jesus Name.

8. I renounce all asthma and bronchial challenges due to elevated levels of pollen and mold in the air. I confess the healing power of your breath and blood over my life.

9. Lord, cause all inflammation rooted in respiratory issues to be neutralized in Jesus Name.

10. I claim diplomatic immunity on all pollution and ozone problems responsible for respiratory system break down in Jesus Name.

11. Father manifest your power in my lungs and air passage way today in Jesus Name. All wheezing, shortness of breath, eczema, dizziness, chest pains, coughing, fatigue and spasms of the airways are bound in Jesus Name.

12. I cover my sinus glands in the blood of Jesus and I decree divine levels of histamine prevail and I am healed of all respiratory flare up's due to sinus problems in the Name of Jesus.

13. I confess redemption from COPD (chronic obstructive pulmonary disease) and its impact upon my

respiratory system in Jesus Name.

14. I forbid any buildup of carbon dioxide in my blood stream during the night. I confess a steady rate of breathing and I renounce all headaches associated with this assignment in Jesus Name.

15. I pray against chronic bronchitis, coughing, build up of mucus and phlegm in my air passageways.

16. I decree I will have healthy breathing patterns and exhale normally. I proclaim rest in Jesus over all tiredness and fatigue which affect my breathing in Jesus Name.

17. I decree healing over any and all lung damage due to emphysema. I claim redemption from this evil disease by the stripes of Jesus Christ.

18. I decree no air will be trapped in my lungs because of emphysema and I

will exhale properly in Jesus Name.

19. I decree there will be no unwholesome affects upon my heart because of respiratory system related issues in Jesus Name.

20. I confess immunity over all acute bronchitis that would cause sudden infections and viruses. I decree robust activity in my lungs in Jesus Name.

21. I renounce all genetic related respiratory problems connected to Cystic Fibrosis. I speak demise and utter ruin upon this infirmity. I decree the blood of Jesus supersedes and super imposes Cystic Fibrosis in Jesus Name.

22. Lord heal my lungs, esophagus, bronchial tubes, air passages ways, the lining of my lungs, throat tissues and entire respiratory system in Jesus Name.

Prayers, Decrees & Confessions for Healing of the Digestive System

1. I proclaim excellence of health and proper functioning in my digestive system.

2. I decree any parasitic issues affecting my intestines are rooted out and burned by the fire of God in the Name of Jesus.

3. Father I ask you to manifest your healing power throughout my entire digestive system. I invoke the supernatural power of the blood of Jesus in my stomach, the lining of my stomach and gut.

4. I decree healing both in my small intestine, large intestine and colon in the Name of Jesus. I command all illegal attachments and unhealthy bacteria to pass through.

5. Lord release your power throughout my digestive tract and heal me in Jesus Name.

6. I proclaim healing from any symptoms rooted in the digestive tract in Jesus Name.

7. I renounce any bleeding, bloating, constipation and any issues with diarrhea in the Name of Jesus.

8. I renounce all stomach and gut related problems connected to my intestine in the Name of Jesus.

9. I command divine healing and divine order to superimpose all digestive tract problems unknown and undiagnosed in the Name of Jesus.

10. Father I invoke your healing power in my GI tract and I proclaim victory over all digestive disorders in Jesus Name.

11. I decree the stripes of Christ empower me to overcome all disease in Jesus Name.

12. I renounce all pain and physical challenges associated with Gastroesophageal Reflux disease, Gallstones, Crohn's disease, Ulcerative Colitis, Irritable Bowel Syndrome, Hemorrhoids and Diverticulitis in Jesus Name.

13. Lord heal me of all abdominal pains and chronic stomach problems in Jesus Name.

14. I decree power over any and all forms of colon and stomach cancer in Jesus Name.

15. I decree no cancer cells shall live in my digestive system. I decree the blood of Jesus powerfully eradicated this disease in Jesus Name.

Prayers, Decrees & Confessions of Healing for the Immune System

1. Father I thank you for your supernatural power working throughout my immune system.

2. I renounce all sickness and disease known to attack the immune system. I decree my body is off limits in Jesus Name.

3. I decree all allergies and hay fever issues are rendered ineffective in my body in Jesus Name.

4. I proclaim the Blood of Jesus releases a supernatural boost in my immune system and my body is supernaturally fighting off all infections, fevers and infirmity.

5. I proclaim divine order and divine synergy between all the systems of my body.

6. I decree there will be no attacks on healthy tissues in my body due to Lupus in the Name of Jesus.

7. I renounce any blood disorders that would cause my immune system to be compromised in Jesus Name!

8. I declare healing over flu like symptoms connected to a sore throat, fever and constant fatigue.

9. I decree my body maintains its proper weight and I am loosed from all sudden weight loss.

10. I come out of agreement with all infections, night sweats and abdominal pains as a result of a compromised immune system. I invoke the stripes of Christ as I decree healing is manifesting in me now.

11. I decree my body harnesses healthy cells which combat and effectively defeat every disease and foreign species seeking to infiltrate my body in Jesus Name.

12. I proclaim excellent cell health. I decree my red and white blood cells are properly aligned with your divine plan for my health in Jesus Name!

13. I renounce Type 1 diabetes and any influence it would have on my immune system.

14. I pray for a balance release of sugar in my blood and a proper discharge through regulated urination in Jesus Name.

15. I renounce all assignments of hell that would seek to destroy my health through a weakened and compromised immune system in Jesus Name.

16. I decree there will be no cell mutation in my body. I forbid this activity in the Name of Jesus.

Prayers, Decrees & Confessions of Healing for the Endocrine System

1. Father I thank you for healing power and divine regularity being loosed upon all the glands of my body.

2. I decree hormonal balance and I command no over or under production of hormonal secretions into the systems of my body in Jesus Name.

3. Lord I thank you that my blood and circulatory system are properly balanced with my endocrine system.

4. I declare my cortisol levels are balanced and will not malfunction in Jesus Name.

5. I cover my adrenal gland in the blood of Jesus and proclaim supernatural order for adequate production of cortisol.

6. I renounce Cushing's Disease Syndrome that would have a negative impact upon my Endocrine System and cause dysfunction in my cortisol levels in Jesus Name.

7. I renounce all hypertension and high blood pressure related issues that may be working against the demise of my health.

8. Lord reveal all irregularities connected to unwarranted abdominal weight gain, weak muscles and bones due to glandular problems in Jesus Name.

9. Lord set me free from all skin disorders and poor bone health that are caused by issues in my Endocrine System.

10. Lord release Your healing power upon my thyroid glands. Heal me from all disorders that would cause this gland to malfunction.

11. I renounce hypo thyroidism that would cause my thyroid gland to fail in producing enough thyroxin.

12. I command divine levels of energy to break forth and all tiredness, shortness of breath and chest pains to leave me in Jesus Name.

13. I command my body to be rid of all demonic influences rooted in hypo thyroidism. Cold hands, cold feet, brittle nails, muscle cramps, digestion problem and water retention issues.

14. Women Only - I renounce any menstrual problems, irregularities with cycle and fertility problems in Jesus Name.

15. I decree the blood of Jesus prevails on my behalf against all headaches, migraines, sinus infections, post nasal drip, visual disturbances, respiratory infections, heart

palpitations, difficulty swallowing, sleep disturbances and bladder problems.

16. I pray against Raynaud's Syndrome and any affects it would have upon my Endocrine System in Jesus Name.

17. I command all allergies, mood swings, heart problems, tumors memory loss and fears associated with Raynaud's Syndrome to leave me in Jesus Name.

18. I claim redemptive power over Raynaud's Syndrome through the blood of Jesus.

19. Lord release Your fire into my adrenal glands and burn both known and unknown disorders.

20. I command every hormone secreting gland to come into divine order. I decree I will not live by the dictates of infirmity in Jesus Name.

21. I speak divine regulation in my thyroid glands and decree any assignments of hyperthyroidism is neutralized by the blood of Jesus.

22. Lord release Your fire and burn any affects of Graves disease that would cause hyperthyroidism.

23. I command any types of diabetes that would seek to breach my health to die in Jesus Name. I renounce all generational and hereditary diabetes in Jesus Name.

24. Father release a divine reset into my metabolic system. Cause my body to properly extract the energy resources I need from the food that I eat in Jesus Name.

25. All abnormal chemical reactions are divinely displaced and my digestive system is operating at optimal levels. I command my liver and pancreas to participate and function properly in Jesus Name.

Prayers, Decrees & Confessions Of Healing For The Nervous System

1. I decree my nerves and neurons operate synergistically, one with the other in Jesus Name.

2. I cover all my brain waves and cerebral activity in the blood of Jesus and decree there will be no disruptions in Jesus Name.

3. I command the generative power of my mind to function in compliance with its Creator in Jesus Name.

4. Lord cause my BETA brain waves to manifest properly so that my alertness and critical reasoning would serve me well.

5. I renounce all anxiety and panic disorders that would seek to interfere with my ALPHA brain waves to be bound in Jesus Name. I decree I will rest properly and function at keen levels of concentration and clarity.

6. I renounce all inaccuracies with my THETA brain waves. I decree my REM (rapid eye movement) patterns that promote inspiration and normal sleep patterns are in divine order.

7. I decree my DELTA brain waves flow properly and my body naturally engages the deep sleep realm. I forbid any disruptions in Jesus Name.

8. I proclaim the power of God upon my GAMMA brain waves and I confess the Lord instructs my reins. I have insight and capacity to process high levels of information and multi-task with ease in Jesus Name.

9. I renounce all neurological disorders associated with seizures and epileptic activity responsible for abnormal electrical discharges from brain cells in Jesus Name.

10. Lord You were wounded and bruised for me and the chastisement of my peace is upon You. I decree that with Your stripes I'm healed of all pain and diseases associated with the nervous system in Jesus Name.

11. I claim redemptive power upon all my motor and cognitive skills that are affected by nerve related issues.

12. Lord heal me of all progressive nerve issues. I renounce all generational proclivities associated with Parkinson's. I declare I will have proper movement and use of all parts of my body in Jesus Name.

13. I loose the restorative power of God upon my nervous system and decree all degenerative diseases at work to damage or destroy my nerve cells is destroyed in Jesus Name.

14. I confess the blood of Jesus over the protective lining of my nerves.

15. I renounce any symptoms of Multiple Sclerosis, Lupus and Devic disease. I decree my immune system will not be subject to any attacks in Jesus Name.

16. I decree harmony between my brain and muscular system. I declare proper communication between my neurons and muscles. I renounce the spirit of infirmity that works with amyotrophic lateral sclerosis (ALS/Lou Gehrig's) in Jesus Name.

17. Lord You've declared the memory of the just is blessed and the name of the wicked shall rot according to Proverbs 10:7. I declare this over my memory and upon Alzheimer's disease. My memory, both long and short term, are blessed.

18. Lord expose any vascular disorders that would serve as a root cause for deterioration of cerebral health and accurate functionality.

19. I declare Your Lordship over my nervous system and all inherited genetic disorders fail and perish in Jesus Name.

20. I proclaim immunity over all infectious diseases that would affect my nervous system.

Old Testament Healing Scriptures

1. And said, If thou wilt diligently hearken to the voice of the LORD thy God, and wilt do that which is right in his sight, and wilt give ear to his commandments, and keep all his statutes, I will put none of these diseases upon thee, which I have brought upon the Egyptians: for I am the LORD that healeth thee.
(Exodus 15:26)

2. And thou shalt go to thy fathers in peace; thou shalt be buried in a good old age. (Genesis 15:15)

3. And the blood shall be to you for a token upon the houses where ye are: and when I see the blood, I will pass over you, and the plague shall not be upon you to destroy you, when I smite the land of Egypt.
(Exodus 12:13)

4. And ye shall serve the LORD your God, and he shall bless thy bread, and thy water; and I will take sickness away from the midst of thee. [26] There shall nothing cast their young, nor be barren, in thy land: the number of thy days I will fulfil. (Exodus 23:25-26)

5. And the LORD will take away from thee all sickness, and will put none of the evil diseases of Egypt, which thou knowest, upon thee; but will lay them upon all them that hate thee. (Deuteronomy 7:15)

6. And the LORD shall make thee plenteous in goods, in the fruit of thy body, and in the fruit of thy cattle, and in the fruit of thy ground, in the land which the LORD sware unto thy fathers to give thee.
(Deuteronomy 28:11)

7. Turn again, and tell Hezekiah the captain of my people, Thus saith the LORD, the God of David thy father, I have heard thy prayer, I have seen

thy tears: behold, I will heal thee: on the third day thou shalt go up unto the house of the Lord. (2 Kings 20:5)

8. I will extol thee, O Lord; for thou hast lifted me up, and hast not made my foes to rejoice over me. ² O Lord my God, I cried unto thee, and thou hast healed me. (Psalm 30:1-2)

9. The Lord will give strength unto his people; the Lord will bless his people with peace. (Psalm 29:11)

10. The Lord will preserve him, and keep him alive; and he shall be blessed upon the earth: and thou wilt not deliver him unto the will of his enemies.
(Psalm 41:2)

11. The Lord will strengthen him upon the bed of languishing: thou wilt make all his bed in his sickness. (Psalm 41:3)

12. There shall no evil befall thee, neither shall any plague come nigh thy dwelling. (Psalm 91:10)

13. With long life will I satisfy him, and shew him my salvation.
(Psalm 91:16)

14. Who forgiveth all thine iniquities; who healeth all thy diseases;
(Psalm 103:3)

15. He sent his word, and healed them, and delivered them from their destructions.
(Psalm 107:20)

16. I shall not die, but live, and declare the works of the Lord.
(Psalm 118:17)

17. He healeth the broken in heart, and bindeth up their wounds.
(Psalm 147:3)

18. It shall be health to thy navel, and marrow to thy bones. (Proverbs 3:8)

19. For they are life unto those that find them, and health to all their flesh. (Proverbs 4:22)

20. Pleasant words are sweet to your soul and health to your bones. (Proverbs 16:24)

21. And the eyes of them that see shall not be dim, and the ears of them that hear shall hearken. (Isaiah 32:3)

22. Then the eyes of the blind shall be opened, and the ears of the deaf shall be unstopped. (Isaiah 35:5)

23. O Lord, by these things men live, and in all these things is the life of my spirit: so wilt thou recover me, and make me to live. (Isaiah 38:16)

24. Surely he hath borne our griefs, and carried our sorrows: yet we did esteem him stricken, smitten of God, and afflicted. 5 But he was wounded for our transgressions, he was bruised for our iniquities: the chastisement of our peace was upon him; and with his stripes we are healed. (Isaiah 53:4-5)

25. I have seen his ways, and will heal him: I will lead him also, and restore comforts unto him and to his mourners.
(Isaiah 57:18)

26. For I will restore health unto thee, and I will heal thee of thy wounds, saith the LORD; because they called thee an Outcast, saying, This is Zion, whom no man seeketh after.
(Jeremiah 30:17)

27. Behold, I will bring it health and cure, and I will cure them, and will reveal unto them the abundance of peace and truth. (Jeremiah 33:6)

New Testament Healing Scriptures

1. That it might be fulfilled which was spoken by Esaias the prophet, saying, Himself took our infirmities, and bare our sicknesses. (Matthew 8:17)

2. But when Jesus heard that, he said unto them, They that be whole need not a physician, but they that are sick. (Matthew 9:12)

3. And Jesus went forth, and saw a great multitude, and was moved with compassion toward them, and he healed their sick. (Matthew 14:14)

4. And Jesus went about all Galilee, teaching in their synagogues, and preaching the gospel of the kingdom, and healing all manner of sickness and all manner of disease among the people. (Matthew 4:23)

5. I went about all cities and villages, teaching in their synagogues and preaching the gospel of the Kingdom and healing every sickness and every disease among the people. (Matthew 9:35)

6. And when he had called unto him his twelve disciples, he gave them power against unclean spirits, to cast them out, and to heal all manner of sickness and all manner of disease. (Matthew 10:1)

7. But when Jesus knew it, he withdrew himself from thence: and great multitudes followed him, and he healed them all; (Matthew 12:15)

8. And besought him that they might only touch the hem of his garment: and as many as touched were made perfectly whole. (Matthew 14:36)

9. And were beyond measure astonished, saying, He hath done all

things well: he maketh both the deaf to hear, and the dumb to speak. (Mark 7:37)

10. My anointing heals the brokenhearted and delivers the captives recovers sight to the blind, and sets at liberty those that are bruised (Luke 4:18)

11. Then he called his twelve disciples together, and gave them power and authority over all devils, and to cure diseases. (Luke 9:1)

12. And the people, when they knew it, followed him: and he received them, and spake unto them of the kingdom of God, and healed them that had need of healing. (Luke 9:11)

13. And they departed, and went through the towns, preaching the gospel, and healing every where. (Luke 9:6)

14. I am not come to destroy men's lives but to save them. (Luke 9:56)

15. Behold, I give unto you power to tread on serpents and scorpions, and over all the power of the enemy: and nothing shall by any means hurt you. (Luke 10:19)

16. And ought not this woman, being a daughter of Abraham, whom Satan hath bound, lo, these eighteen years, be loosed from this bond on the sabbath day? (Luke 13:16)

17. And it came to pass on a certain day, as he was teaching, that there were Pharisees and doctors of the law sitting by, which were come out of every town of Galilee, and Judaea, and Jerusalem: and the power of the Lord was present to heal them. (Luke 5:17)

18. And he sent them to preach the kingdom of God, and to heal the sick. (Luke 9:2)

19. And heal the sick that are therein, and say unto them, The kingdom of God is come nigh unto you. (Luke 10:9)

20. In him was life; and the life was the light of men. (John 1:4)

21. The thief cometh not, but for to steal, and to kill, and to destroy: I am come that they might have life, and that they might have it more abundantly. (John 10:10)

22. Jesus said unto her, I am the resurrection, and the life: he that believeth in me, though he were dead, yet shall he live: (John 11:25)

23. By stretching forth thine hand to heal; and that signs and wonders may be done by the name of thy holy child Jesus.
(Acts 4:30)

24. And Peter said unto him, Aeneas, Jesus Christ maketh thee whole: arise, and make thy bed. And he arose immediately.
(Acts 9:34)

25. How God anointed Jesus of Nazareth with the Holy Ghost and with power: who went about doing good, and healing all that were oppressed of the devil; for God was with him.
(Acts 10:38)

26. Christ hath redeemed us from the curse of the law, being made a curse for us: for it is written, Cursed is every one that hangeth on a tree:
(Galatians 3:13)

27. Wherefore lift up the hands which hang down, and the feeble knees; [13] And make straight paths for your feet, lest that which is lame be turned out of the way; but let it rather be healed. (Hebrews 12:12-13)

28. Confess your faults one to another, and pray one for another, that ye may be healed. The effectual fervent prayer of a righteous man availeth much. (James 5:16)

29. Who his own self bare our sins in his own body on the tree, that we, being dead to sins, should live unto righteousness: by whose stripes ye were healed. (1 Peter 2:24)

30. Beloved, I wish above all things that thou mayest prosper and be in health, even as thy soul prospereth. (3 John 2)

More Great Resources from Apostle Stephen A. Garner

Books
- Apostolic Pioneering
- Benefits of Praying in Tongues
- Essentials of the Prophetic
- Exposing the Spirit of Anger
- Fundamentals of Deliverance 101, Revised & Expanded
- Ministering Spirits: "Engaging the Angelic Realm"
- Pray Without Ceasing, Special Edition
- Restoring Prophetic Watchmen
- Deliver Us From Evil
- Prayers That Strengthen Marriages & Families
- Prayers, Decrees & Confessions for Goodness & Mercy
- Prayers, Decrees & Confessions for Wisdom
- Prayers, Decrees & Confessions for Favour & Grace
- Prayers, Decrees & Confessions for Righteousness
- Prayers, Decrees & Confessions for Prosperity
- Prayers, Decrees & Confessions for Increase
- Prayers, Decrees & Confessions for Rewards
- Prayers, Decrees & Confessions for Peace
- Prayers, Decrees & Confessions for Power
- Strife the Enemy of Advancement

CD's
- Prayers For The Nations
- Prayers Against Python &.Witchcraft
- Prayers Of Healing & Restoration
- Thy Kingdom Come
- Overcoming Spirits of Terrorism
- Songs of Intercession
- The Spirit of the Breaker

**Visit Our Online Ministry Bookstore @ www.sagministries.com
Email: sagarnerministries@gmail.com**

Made in the USA
Columbia, SC
10 September 2017